Copyright © 2021 Colleen Chapman

All rights reserved. Without prior permission of the authors, no part of this publication may be reproduced, stored in a retrieval system, or transmitted in any form or by any means— electronic, mechanical, photocopy, recording, or any other— except for brief quotations in printed reviews.

ISBN: 978-1-7348258-7-9 (Paperback)
978-1-7348258-8-6 (Hardback)
978-1-7348258-9-3 (Ebook)

Library of Congress Control Number: 2021923350

Illustrations by Ananta Mohanta
Book Design by Praise Saflor

Publisher's Cataloging-in-Publication data

Names: Chapman, Colleen, author. | Mohanta, Ananta, illustrator.
Title: Buffy and Sissy go on a road trip / by Colleen Chapman; illustrated by Ananta Mohanta.
Series: The Traveling Kittens
Description: Blaine, WA: Colleen Chapman, 2021. | Summary: Join the Traveling Kittens, Buffy and Sissy on their family road trip where they camp, visit exciting places and even meet a cowboy!
Identifiers: LCCN: 2021923350 | ISBN: 978-1-7348258-8-6 (hardcover) | 978-1-7348258-7-9 (paperback) | 978-1-7348258-9-3 (ebook)
Subjects: LCSH Kittens--Juvenile fiction. | Automobile travel--Juvenile fiction. | Camping--Juvenile fiction. | CYAC Kittens--Fiction. | Automobile travel--Fiction. | Camping--Fiction. | BISAC JUVENILE FICTION / Animals / Cats | JUVENILE FICTION / Social Themes / New Experience | JUVENILE FICTION / Travel
Classification: LCC PZ7.1.C484 Buf 2021| DDC [E]--dc23

Buffy & Sissy Go on a Road Trip

Author: Colleen Chapman

Illustrator: Ananta Mohanta

"Kittens, it's time for our road trip!" shouts Mama, pulling up in a shiny white camper van.

"Yay," shout the kittens.

"Can we stay at a motel with a swimming pool?" asks Sissy.

"I want to sleep outside under the stars!" says Buffy.

Early the next morning, everyone is packed and ready to go. The drive is fun for a while, but soon the kittens are hungry and bored.

Sissy asks, "Are we there yet?"

Mama laughs. "Not for a while, but we can stop for snacks."

Back in the van, the kittens eat their snacks and soon fall fast asleep. When they wake up, they see a big sign: Welcome to **Yellowstone National Park**.

"There's OLD FAITHFUL!" says Mama, pointing to a huge spray of water gushing out of the ground. "It's one of the most famous geysers in the world. Can you believe it erupts twenty times every day?"

Standing a safe distance away, Sissy takes a selfie with OLD FAITHFUL in the background.

Nearby, a moose named Pete tells the kittens about the dangers of forest fires. "It is important to make sure your campfire is completely out, and never play with matches!"

Buffy and Sissy take pictures with Pete. He gives them stickers that name them official park rangers. They promise Pete they won't play with fire.

The kittens are bored on the long drive. They decide to play a game. "Sissy, let's see how many Volkswagen Beetles we can find!" says Buffy. "They are such cute cars. When you find one, say love bug!"

"Look at that big mountain. It has faces on it!" Buffy suddenly shouts. Sissy grabs her camera.

"We are at Mount Rushmore National Park," says Mama. "Those are faces of United States Presidents: George Washington, Thomas Jefferson, Theodore Roosevelt and Abraham Lincoln."

Sissy imagines herself as one of the workers carving the faces on the mountain.

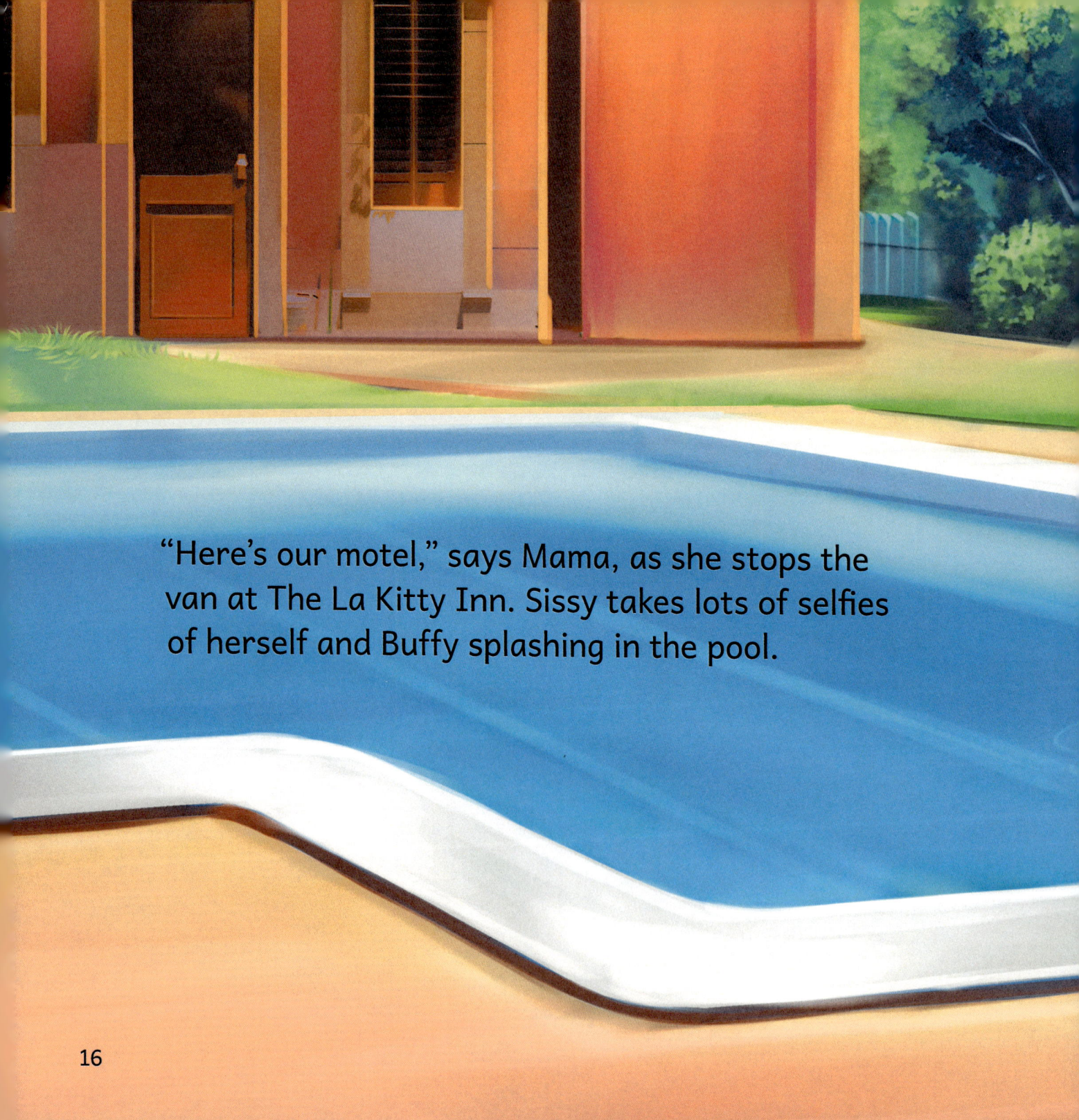

"Here's our motel," says Mama, as she stops the van at The La Kitty Inn. Sissy takes lots of selfies of herself and Buffy splashing in the pool.

As they get ready for bed, Buffy and Sissy run around the hotel room and look for a place to hide. Mama finds them laughing under the bed.

"What's for breakfast and where are we going now?" Buffy asks the next morning.

Mama feeds the kittens their breakfast and says, "We are on our way to a beautiful place!"

"Can we get more snacks for the road?" Asks Buffy.

Everywhere they look, the kittens see huge red rocks unlike anything they have ever seen.

"Mama, where are we?" Buffy asks, as Sissy takes photo after photo.

"We are in Arches National Park in Utah," Mama answers.

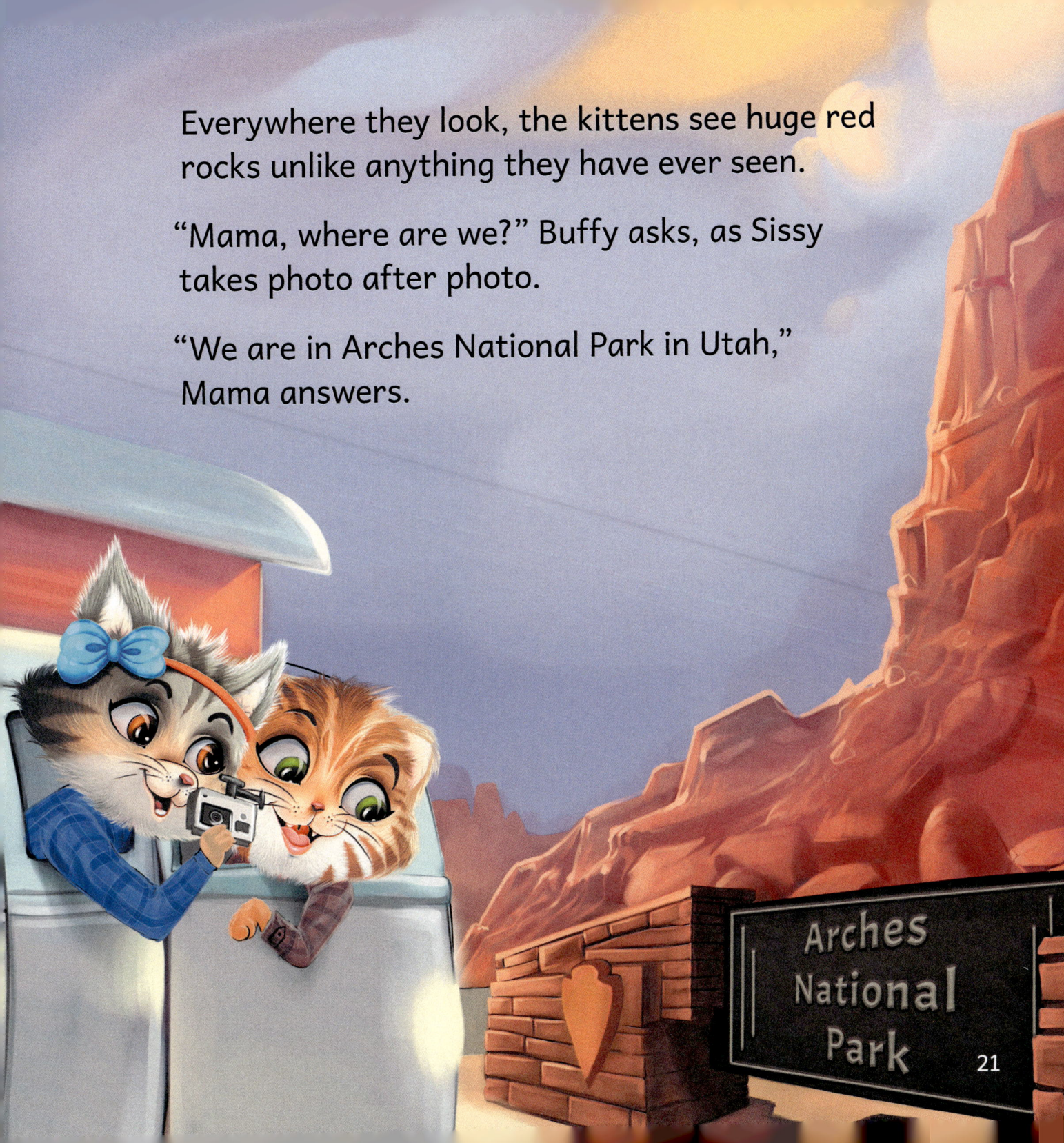

"This is a magical world of red rocks," says Sissy. Buffy is so excited, she doesn't even complain about being hungry.

Mama tells the kittens, "this park has over 2000 arches made of stone."

That evening, Mama parks the van at a campsite and the kittens sleep outside under the stars. They set up their sleeping bags next to the campfire and make s'mores from graham crackers, melted marshmallows and chocolate.

"This is now officially my favorite food," says Buffy, as she learns to create a perfectly-cooked marshmallow.

"Mine are all burnt," says a frustrated Sissy.

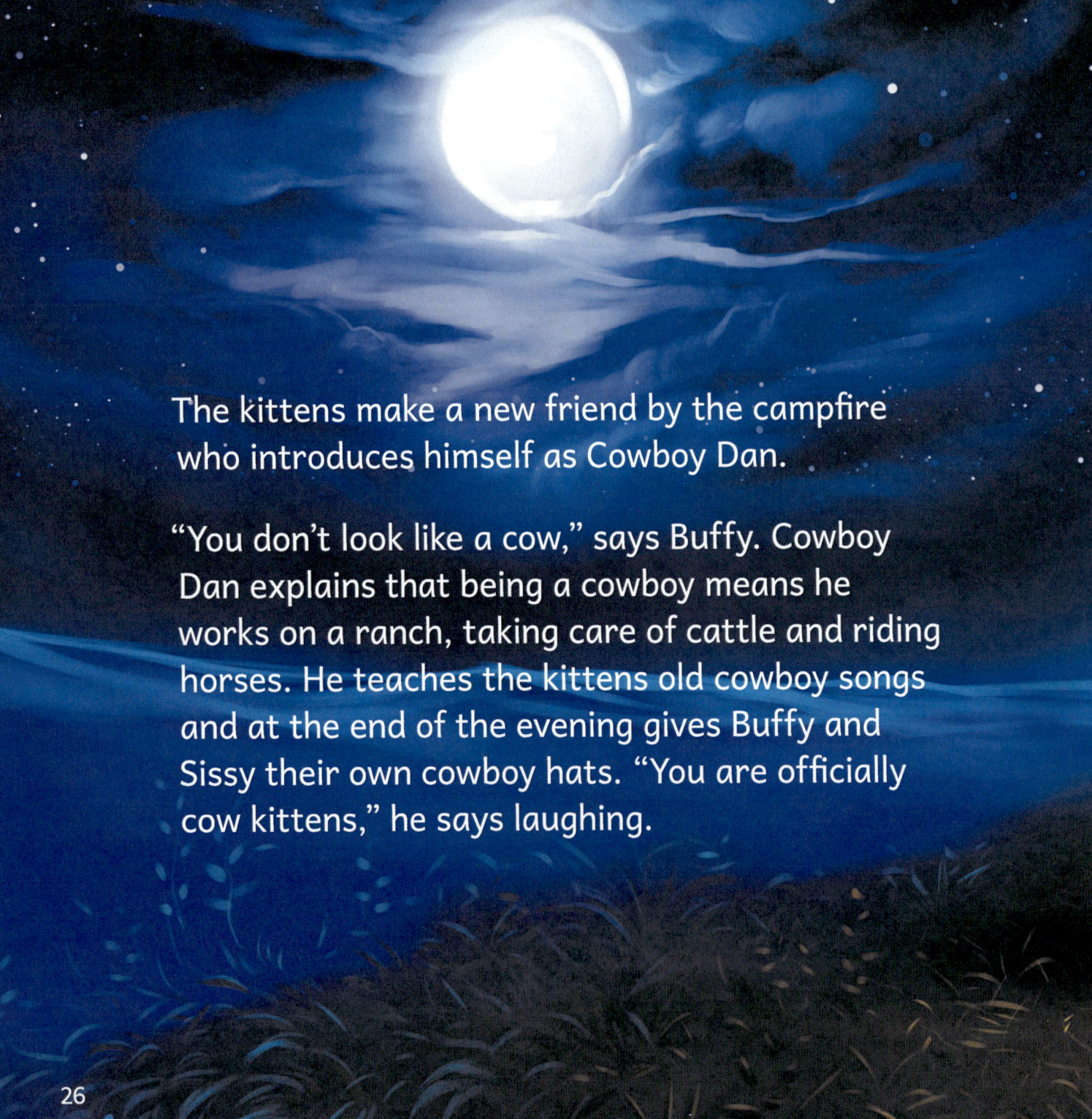

The kittens make a new friend by the campfire who introduces himself as Cowboy Dan.

"You don't look like a cow," says Buffy. Cowboy Dan explains that being a cowboy means he works on a ranch, taking care of cattle and riding horses. He teaches the kittens old cowboy songs and at the end of the evening gives Buffy and Sissy their own cowboy hats. "You are officially cow kittens," he says laughing.

The kittens crawl into their sleeping bags. Soon Sissy is fast asleep while Buffy watches the shooting stars.

When they get home, the kittens reminisce about their trip.

Sissy says, "My favorite memory is singing with Cowboy Dan and sleeping under the stars."

Buffy says, "I loved seeing Old Faithful and eating s'mores."

As the kittens help unpack the van, they give Mama big hugs and thank her for taking them on the road trip.

They look forward to their next adventure. Where will it be?

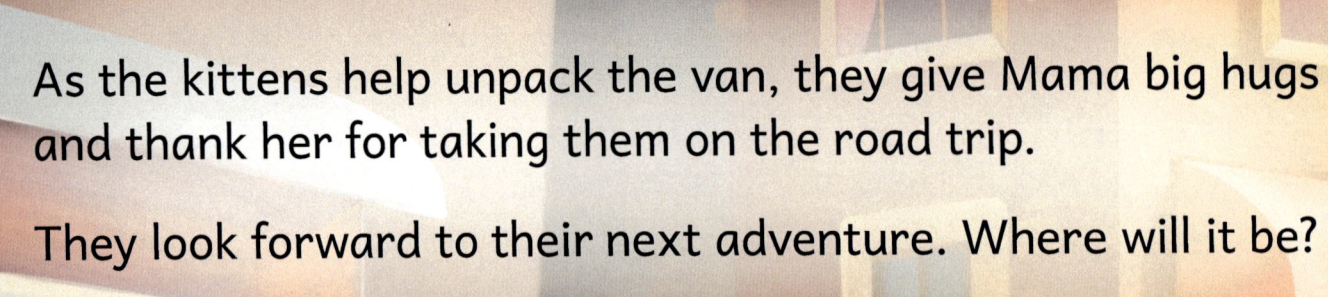

Please visit **www.thetravelingkittens.com** to download your free activity and coloring sheets of

Buffy and Sissy Go on a Road Trip

Follow Buffy & Sissy on social media!

YouTube https://bit.ly/3DaZc2Q

Instagram thetravelingkittens2

Facebook The Traveling Kittens

Giving back is important to Buffy & Sissy. A portion of the profits of this series will go towards charities to help animals.

Share this book with your friends!

Made in the USA
Middletown, DE
15 December 2021